OCLOCK

Mary Rising Higgins

POTES & POETS PRESS
Elmwood CT
2000

"Eight PM" was first published as
"Eight o' Clock Mesa" in *red table(S*
La Alameda Press (Albuquerque, 1999).

To those who patiently listened and read with me
during the workings of *oclock*:
Jeff Bryan, Sharon DiMaria,
Kathleen Linnell, Maryhelen Snyder,
Phyllis Thompson, and Dora Wang.
I want to say thank you.
Once again, I am especially grateful to Gene Frumkin,
Sheila E. Murphy, and John Tritica
for careful readings and suggestions.
Special thanks to my sister, who helps find time.

Cover art: *pinhole photographs,* Mary Rising Higgins

Cover design: J. Bryan.

Second Printing

ISBN 1-893541-25-8

Printed by Van Volumes Ltd

printed in the U. S. A.

for further information please write:
Potes & Poets Press Inc
181 Edgemont Avenue
Elmwood CT 06110-1005

oclock

for D. R.

where to rightward
explain leaves out
thought bog   eye blink   flashecho
slim shaft pulse we drive to catch and sling
mulltip words at a tabled hour
what is your theory of now
works toward us to draw memory
in walk through thoughts
borrowed words rearrange
at the neutral boundaries of
urban siren sprawlscape harp
under the skin of frozen water
flight wings edge

ELEVEN AM

for FM

List art, day motion, fire frame. Where a girl might move from the habit of silence, gesture blossoms gold-tongued practice. Honeysuckle trellis idioms mime. Persona repetitions please. Blank pages take the breath possible, where a number to enter makes sense of each awe gamut twist, flawless conscription. Outside children suspend themselves in hide and seek. To track each moment floods a mirror for time. Polished and constant where time expects her. Whorl story. Ear shell enclosure. A pleasing station to which game could be driven, the hunt disguised in silk purse override where survival collides a body out of four corner resist, marked calends pace

toward first
day reach
telegraph dress
variant flagstone
edge swerve
anything neglects
along tomorrowed
body valence
hold sail
mountain scent
with meadow grass anchor triggers forgetting

names. Throw words in the air. *Oh the joy of me* climbs a ladder once again, the way house and yard roots remeasure energy then count deeper through unfolding wave battles from underpoem. Along the causeway surface errors a slight thirst desert zinnia asphalt snaps. Customary. Whatever growing. consider not putting out the fire. Ground cover will be gone soon enough and either way looking for more. Back yard waxes under tramline crest range muse. Local sun cools with virga brush. Whatever form will take a bracket where the houseyard calls for that brand-new light shredder. Yellow iris recycle assessment possible briefly before each whipped stitch

plied stretch lattice
work site
heat blot

permit place
unattended blue
jet slam
precisely radiant
polymer moment
rain crib
mulch scatter
extend scraps

familiar soon with other striations, the leisure to say what comes after. Again which day this draws into slight open window siffle, then eaves arch rain torrent deluge. Sound thickness not just another action cranked open to violet blooms and bug screen track toward afternoon hungerweather, where out of the yard they kept safe for lizard, bird, and snake, three giant cholla wait, chopped to haul on a truck bed. They cling in mesh-stunned familiar life hold after long thriving through dry heat undone by chancy rain. Their last dropped needles bend to stalker cats and new concrete over herbicide in forward shift velocity detail plastic shelves condition like anything else. To think she has been this already underway listens from

sustain flight
back forth
conscription spokes
risk laced
wake boundary
migrant life
onsite stores
excursion piece
concave gradient
tune out

fenestral evidence, neighborhood beat slam. Face the grain of air swung sleek in breathhold sky groomed winter sun slides brisk unscudded. Grip bolts now never although dim waves align a small shelled beach, the art of gray pout day practice downy reach expanding then. Shall privileged, for example, an I-shaped life. Inscape reforms tools or weapons if we agree to start here phonetic resift she thinks from. Well meanings to arrive from before this one, and no other words for cancellation range toward day premise, dream formation. What will she ask points to one another. As what if you train yourself in the art of no not these requirings, in the spark of starting out, as morning plums cast. We devour fierce filings of then again's varied wobble

served where
no other
means to
days later
mind flare
what if
bell booted
gong rest
clock pull

repetition a returning note where sand skin beads deflect water. Cool dipping to bear the mind. Mood collage range focus in yesterday options held in traveled brass. Birthday completion vessels another snug fiction practice. Same roof the wealthrose, the hummingbird darts. Previous prepares coarse nectar plaiting however home thoughts on familiar tapes feel. Knot dreams cluster and bank. Lectern sound quilts where phonemes waft her what did you think before daze length hold line filter as you expect switch stasis end planting speech pieces together according resolute breath vertices. Carry what early strata entail from high storm wind signals in a series of chest taps meaning seed leaf exponents reduce us

conclusion ruins
spur to
flat line
foot note
hunter noon
index practice
season whisper
chanting toward

bound universe
check this rework balance discard day
knot quoting headlong slide pulse in ruddy arc echo, listen
awash in erase traffic slowed by sage pool perpendicular to
event shadow, attention touch by what means and some days
only. Without escape span opposites situate perfectly. Wheat
straw sung into clay wheel body laps long and furious warm
the footpath to more precise feeling. Last year's corners neatly
pin nothing enough exhibit airy locust side motion to little
heart feet morning ferries midline into found personality
hymns. With slight hesitations she tells you what you want in
things let fall, stretch, clutter, time animation light shaped
after sketched patterns consolation requires. Everyday blocks
from transparent type
flash silk
pass hand
to hand
feeder birds
perch chirp
slant praise
fat bobbed
juniper needles
broom feathered
window tap flight zone handbook view
walks beneath wind-trimmed poplars, past the gate's blue paint
coat dotted with red finch cap. Sometimes planning what she
means as temperatures reach at last entry exit with no string
hang simplicity or fence cornered wind sweep acquaintance
with letting go in just a bit of how misunderstandings repeat
us. The way we've done it agendas industrious with soothing
dread on the water constructs these puzzles she might wish
through thread wrappings to rest across dreaming uneven
numbers, a form of accusation told in somewhere absence
wells, and no one else to look out for rain curled leaf change
reliquaries cloud lit precisely to more new sense repairs in
october roofing
another year

burned memories
warm slate
body climb
far from
this bog
tar paper
folds torn
on and on only when driven in
patient music. Surrounding air tastes of prairie sage and groundcherry subtext off coast remembers along quote touch pose erasure, although extravagance of late turned cottonwood after first freeze continuum in brilliant leaf clatter inhabits work toward noon. The rest of the day safely doing nothing despite late waking in a nest burrowed out of switched percentages danced across xeric water plans lain white trim to the glass table out back where particular steps require her like so much dust and clutter visible at the hour's angle. Pulling the handtruck succumbs to gravity. Bisque tiles charm the sunbowl feet. Sometimes too thick to navigate until stunning shine exacts verdance
houseplans invest
destinations arrive
tell fireworks
from gunshots
one way
through float
today's cloudburst
under partly
cloudy sky
missing the garden after 100 degree heat
errands. Conversant day stasis without some book too long waiting, as though lines know where they will go to fold whole cloth. Smoke spire and other ambitions adapt us to feel which traffic goes where. Next week waxing layers with new paint. Occasion to beauty a hobbled inscription like a troubled

drivetrain to repair or exchange. An example to make up the mind, streak splayed bud shoots from whiprooted phlox, ride anchor toward final moment feelings later cut from colored glass unbuttoning thick speech drunk often so we do not hear. Pieceworks of conscience a desperate callousing. Athletic arrow and target with nowhere to change consensus despite this running faster

fickle appreciation
pleasing said
stuck on
middle floor
after hello
tradition experiments
straw bind
required set
expand points
concern for the art of television an actual

expression along with bipartisan fetterings. Said perhaps walking beside one of those girls who has fallen in love with a reflection of being here, though probably not you. Struck silent omissions point deciduous as shades of white frost glass blown to time the last moment in how to live otherwise. Just the way advice furnishes tomorrow from yesterday's clarifying scribble enclosure hatch and feather lines follow to avoid crowd motion in any given dried rose winter filled with speckled starling preen through stalk and prance too-temperate morning between useful moments that let life gel comfortably into plans we make. And who cares what turns around the battered skillet heats refraining

etch stone
claims between
like or
not familiar
ignored overtake
estranging song
birds driven
wayward shift a dizzy topspin after

deep echo underpin pulls crawlspace from abbreviating breath marks. Just as they say, no longer into change what she means, though what if the water were clear, were still. She wanes pup-like in armchair visions while even yellow budding snapdragons carried indoors stretch to peer above a kitchen window ledge. Anything wants new, gravitating from november light locus in circular saw partitioned goose down and weed burned air replacement for aster fields and flame flowers ringing thirsty trees after hurricane edge splash. Larger than life songs practice wanting more as the calendar entails us with raddle tap tighter words for pebble skip knot impatience jam
sustained happens
anyone forgets
tidal biting
intersecting freeze
wind spray
roof slate
approach road
symptoms adjust
vacation calls
you feel no answer cross the shallow for
make up new ways to hear. Okay disguises in what it means later, so you come up short like a space bar lisp lock epidemic where she wakes to face bright notings nobody else agreed to schedule in parts for her, sifting later habit fed ground bubbles to unfold from rain drought slam into upslant fogged forward drag, whatever getting keeps you toward summit till spade work and late cut poppy dividends in siege lever platitudes' double echo. Comet channels fit in with lady hard hats where soccer inroads impel without apparent signing argued or said quite that way somehow clears for a moment without intending. Wild trust overcurrent view hovers. Blinking her eye into orbit moves

NOON

12.00.01 :justified water centers as a pool with steps leading down from

tiles carefully arranged by color and line meaning

clear steep road she thinks she is talking out of
though not here in particular

shadowless
maddog woman altitude dial

upright into the bearable slant of the sun's cleansing eye
cage curve tread breakthrough clean the slate order

fragment aura

orangeyellow streaks the fragrant heliotrope

primed
water drop strike heliosis
plumbline sun altar

spotted leaf sand scorch

meridiation
vacant hour heat magnet

brass ring sun horizon
marked transit circle

meridial orange poppy

midpoint heliogram

nothing to add helioabyss

12.05.02

: tan cloak   pallor dazzle
dreadlocked

sequence of arbitrary

opens as
opportunity takes us

electronic epistemology
announcement in which you arrange

to be recognized amid known clatter
like any wide ring sung
dance grid followed by scottish tenor
heliosphere lofting cold frost morning

where improved temperatures promise
though unable to repeat the territory

storytell definitions ground coarse

as even sacred lists tangle

the means of hope outdoors new limit actions too much whorl for thought and the difficulties of one another trestle hold expectations into the *quaquaversal* of each day's universe from slingshot gravity matrix graceful terror dreams to what extent from grid curve familiar sounds we place despite all the new technowhisper shapes of later hunger all you can eat aftertalk component clarities the way to file keys where are you in storytell winter to bring open time tasks too much action to live right thinks a means of hope indoors as limited action

still the difficulties of one another do I look right to you expects one despite casting about with nothing for where are you filled in by lighted keyboard rhythms while others require standing as hopeful overcasts to matter the shapely landscape and lounge reflects considered intent weight throughout now must act

12.10.03

:~~fragment aura~~

Against sunlight stagger spiked hibiscus eyes half close. High key petals recede in white Braille speech pocks full of herself devoured foregrounds the target range flashlit misread. To what fraction divides body as train sync, as timed notes humming. World mouth start limbs form sounds cipher for how one confuses unsounding interest with stuck in the sentence soap nostalgia. Out of the transit what is left undone signals. Buoyed foraging rights any achievement ceremonies or purchased moment living business toward tomorrows. Calculus never leaves her picturing surface in outreach hands to model what characters short term nature cup ledge buzz draft speed.

Steer axis. Beside the freeway speed limit sign a U-haul trailer opens, under police aim workers packed hands up behind their heads crouch. Dark blue draw in heat field currency before traffic choke meaning we get there in the elasticity of light soaking in the energy without resistance to see things

through

without visible progress

not why not how

she is steady

under

what

rule

go

&

12.15.04

: pebbles collect vagrant white sum
once it happens is

fragments collect to unfold another
sum(mation

adventure lost being
no one pulse exactly like another
though it is counted in similar fashion
music stage

sound brake and push
from the shape of this moment release in ascent to

sulfur breath city dissipates   while time wraps us in full
don't stand so close to me where romantic constructions pass
an intersection of special phases underwritten

where does consonance
dissonance to
spacewrap

where noon lies on the meridian
high key image

flash lit misread white zone

12.20.05

: firewalk apogee
solarium
wicker work cage pace

myth foregrounds us as
split hesitation point
to illustrate
sun yoke   water slant   color apex

silhouette box
empty motion between parallels
although logic resist considers a thing certain

dowry turf slide and carry across redefinition

sunstone reliquary

where nothing overshadows

12.25.06

: life standing in
cloudcap tapers
shield by stages to
knot the invisible

expect what is expected knows this
how we choose in off-rack life
to fold this way or that

shapes only as you provide necessity
an I centers in the smell of nicotine
smoke scents my curled and hennaed hair

how fast can you of into above between after
let the fire decide when in the

become me as beloved palindrome
summer warms beyond the
burst float periphery singing overhead

half flowers and veil arrange the orbit slope
feeling our way out of the landfill
the only way to be sure

full-lit moment everything

calls attention to itself
too comfortable and full
backs against the pocked wall

we pillow
I am so bad for you
and on you turn

glutted air around me burns
to ignite the waiting cold
I know you through how you

to be so should
nothing times this when no
first hand accounts go there

turn away in blue frame light and
what have you explosions
ox void eyes and slow hair

lean against the cushion
each ringed finger pretending hunger poses
a next millennium offset

pinholed trace point interfering moon
paper cast white gown
eclipse penumbras

12.30.07

: as often it means before arriving
how he stands amid seedy primrose
smoke draws whose attention to his mouth
though lines of the photograph eliminate
much disquietude leading up to a white flare
eye facets mediate sunlit mechanisms
clouds read from left weather motion
spectrachoke postcards upright
while the season's declination offers
ice light
vacant apogee
motion between concurs

aspect of theory without remainder
beyond same breath energies
fan charm to sweep away overcast
frost funnelled winds
divert attention of the gods

default becomes she   yes, she   begins always this palimpsest

12.35.08

: enjambed flowers nod

uncolonized idea waver

tinfoil truck drive   future perfect progressive of *to be*

laughter past rage high desert heat

break free surface after so many hands reach

self)comfort monologue steps back further
along rooster strut talk where not like the news but a young girl with matches and sand
contour with other pleasing targets predator function recycles preparation for

the point covers everything
choose one of two
a way to polish most light axis

polishing a livid white of attar

bird sweep rush startle

scrabble rocket
trick moves and ghosts inhabit
where even fish schools wheel

distortion glass world look bruised winter mountains
feeling harbor
litter landscape with house repetitions

auditory patents pend
because you are
because you are not
the precise number of steps required

rhinestone and plastic begging bowls the
gaudy rectangles plead
while heavy hands explain their
territory replace in the work
pinprick stars constellate lively vacuum

12.40.09

: preparing to

and other intentionals

explain where you are in charge of why

Mira into

mainstream wait and buy it

solar flare

when I curl up I feel bitter in the space between we mean

spots when I close my eyes

where do you talk from in everything's okay

cute icon duologue and nouns gender

sunlit mood elevator

each day hands down in fine black lines on ivory

creates a parallel *to be*

pretty enough in his long leather jacket and hoopring ears but afterward what will he say grooming brilliant plumage still in love with needle brush stroke quilled sharp enough to pierce my tongue. Do we touch other in our reflex scratch marked tree hold sun power locked up *et ceteras*, and how to agree on erotic others as additive list. Greenleaf registries adhere to twig work recycling a recent corner petroleum glows

12.45.10

: solstice in the body energy cycles out of sync sleep patterns not about the dark hunger patterns not about food season lag winter lag planetary lag today I am as alive as I ever was occasions being caught up where she hums along disclusion although depression aesthetics and other descriptors sentiment I recognize the desert of your dream the given voice shapes by life in far enough away to say I editing also memory with the usual blank surprises

take it

from each other as I watch you talk to yourself another power dirge along fierce benign growth then double tongues heat drawn opposites freeze reasonable woman standards differ by law the average person's space is three feet go further with explanatory suffixes arranged to demonstrate a childhood spongebrush in which colors place the image far enough away to say this

birth gives in toward nurturing whatever the world's rain across a terrain of disclude example courage in a crosshair of speech the instant is written though daily variants unfold attention persona slantwork toward the obliquities of a noun from which she erases obliquities of here to understand the history of her and other jumps to community must be understood in this context

12.50.11

: landfill stars

we write the empty spaces

open to later hunger winds

into gray layer day

repetition downway wings build

edible effigies

cliff jump

iris fictions the word still

despite new difficulties

thought for action much too indoors as familiar place after curb trip speech backs away from oncoming traffic the smells of wet carburetor

side effects for no reason mood lift

region drunk expression and holds to

opposite distilled of expectation until

the point covers everything

wound shape music   a)historical spoons play differently

woodbone and steel

to let it know something

where long ago might hear him   she speaks to herself

12.55.12

: breath hold heat

effects based targeting remodels intention and fragments lace flash cradle listers across a perpendicular. Moment love swing range limits not as emotion. Pencil in midday light wake, it's all morning. Simple can and can't do thinks anew by resonate fixed lay ins to establish a root by sections. Poisoned starlings in winter plumage struggle in the grass. Local sun collapses. Two second occurrence arcs go out as *kevorkian* with passing operatic moments. Undertake us by ringnail picked straight and clear where ambition

or preparation set apart. Refuse our helpless need of one another. Conceal wordless rage by humming. Monologued brain imbalance explains chemistry running away from underthought and overthought crosshatch. Pace decorative floral motif in gothic dried blood calligraphy or this year's traditional approach. After emotion and should domains logic surface, not exactly how it feels but how it looks when she stops laughing and laughing over sewn up points of light for the privileged to observe under a bell in sleep's deep gravity. Somewhere must have heard it in mummed silence, perhaps when the freeway merge phone rings to answer escapes into exaltation. Life, movies, youth mentored by youth, boxing around personal argument a reverence for same old beauty killbox shorthands

helios

breath altar

reflex wake

aftermath brood

ONE PM

power tea boil at which cubicle and other periodic
withdrawals on account never too thin for tv lighting
levels into the long crumhorn afternoon begins to sound
not encouraging but resolute we have always ourselves
to dread rock cling collapses into the business of
loquacions left to remember things all over the place
with small talk batter's exhausting conversational
labored habit's anvil case placing which face second
discourse and how many faces make a whole story
where correct endings disclose the unapparent choices

certain colors bind decor community a nice idea and it's
a ball moving though tired of being thought by telltale
gaps which have nothing to do with you progressing on
parallel tracks for ring dance re-entry though no old
business welcome in how to be there for each other at
specified hour collisions wave out the window we
figure from lives long enough to recover payment for
filling in shadows on those boxes arranged like steps a
wilderness made to look like it holds the water inside
this vase with resin tulip we'll continue to swim beside

screen fish look back epiphanies we are amazed by
desires we forget climbing gracious cruelties lives work
through slipshod speed turn up across circuit board huff

and puff nothing shouts louder speaking to choirs and
onsite destruction fierce brands of personality colonize
where is that thickening agent we expected to chew
with we will work out what you're looking at in show
me series net edit preference advance proxies direct
return empty headed to the place it has been select
names among those at a distance applied to message

responses where hear what I wanted picks up not sitar
but tuning though one way stops us amid factoid array
seesaw intimidation where west pillaging east turns
intercom crackle sputter under dreadful prism strobes
not an easy happiness what happens next chooses the
arrangement and how much per hour life costs to buy
frames that look like they have substance clever hurry
centers now between points and the between-point's
boundary break who drives this world music mindrift
raucous birds and hand shake edges around the platter

where straw votes don't scratch the surface overbuild
millennium city desert aquifer sinkholes raze by black
chrome angle searchlight eat at the desk to leave early
here while office southwest staccato chief number four
east bound one thirty departure runs late move on to
see what that seep range means when jogging in and out
of fast lane slow lane wherever doesn't have to be the
same thing for who drives that made in america truck
tinted windows high bed for slow turn fast roll easy
enough to relocate under urban kite catch wire

drought spring blueheat dustfog rises to the roof of the mouth *dear L* where only to ask differs from no one there depending on how you place yourself according to shredded paper mulch print intrigues for long hall side door hour entry wednesday very likely cancels night list check off circles relax sift a constellating capital of lines where slow down in thought goes without saying seat of the pants and enough to get us through bail out quandaries informed examples file to a number of figures probabilities two in which to mean

programming how long is fun supposed toward silver choke lines fragile development builds you come from whatever sticks in your head daily overtime and place differ getting past myself to think at last collects toward unities colliding there *nandina* branch scree-scratches the window and prayerplant dustwarm leaves rattle to bring the water indoors our own doorway where you come from more or less energy shapes necklace tumble everyday seeds the space available must fill who and which movement you include to balance it all conflicts

visions a habit of incomplete breathing adjusted for basket swing logic transit giving signs the sense where you are my *internal property* counts on a way that mongrel dog crawls back under the latest fence dig out off hand properties appose wordsplash view of simple the frontier of how to do it yet another way draws us through redo drift spurs although unreal synapses express me better without obverse literal bios gong technoskin electronic love hover insisting upon suggestion whatever we see around here we do surfaces

disturbance in average flight but very satisfactory with leeches placed behind the ear or along the hour listen for bad luck mistakes tangle in overhead fan stages for that new diet lemonade to make you ready for anything songs drone in just able to afford it chic where the radio dial also places impossible schedules perhaps she muses an interview between her favorite poets contending how life surprises continue in don't read though eating donuts is okay or name the gesture discloses everything in movies we have seen lately so

he'll want to know if you're married sounds red yellow or green cause effect fantasies narrate cradled curve axes means for everyday constraint orders as too many tasks to get the work done no more staring into space nose bite cologne analogies sort middle layers where making connections becomes you as electronic variant under pedestrian light slab flicker producing never at home ecocenters in midvoice job conduction overlays with assumption event toward opposites keep-talking tomorrow trends in quick shift culture display

Two PM

start leaving town from landslip retellings hold
on how you look at it with funny visuals
~~muted~~

fixing the I in bumper to bumper discourse
fractals carbon and glass break dance beat fest

to find the necessary referral form restrains
affection entering the image through any place
~~you start~~ *is*

~~how this will~~
meaning not you inscape we detail according
to contrast options daylight begins to set out

~~not a pretty picture although~~
it can be drawn mostly we attack for territory
that looks better than meshwork afterwards

applied voice registers however you see the
past from day care clock hand view crossovers

then let the words on a too white page tell you
how the latest horse struggles to its feet while
~~ready for next climbs on~~

too certain makes life mean differently where
the game keeps changing lines to draw a sense
~~for how to get it right~~

~~just breathe while you talk~~

want approaches trace memories of light on
snow most of the time numbers mean anything

~~how deep improves what~~
copies profit vision range changes key
questions full of your favorite shoreline moves

where silence questions best probably begins
to lake drag deeper though whether that's good
~~or not takes time~~

~~not unlike walking in the rain to let drops~~
strike the face and back someone provides
target homage between fighting spirit hills

job trance flight horizon options a cheerful
crater we landscape according to interior decor
~~we fix on one another~~

~~let go before the hour is up~~
geometries with answers we work from chart
throwaway home life norm tubes ebb and flow

also coordinates calculate what you know in
this venture of just where we thought
~~childhood is over~~

~~we trim thinking everyone~~
does as order to bring the image indoors
though paint on a large mirror may not reflect

where he smiles into the camera focuses on the
dog's face a way to view objects arranged in
~~black and white~~

~~off balance hopper quota~~
other mysteries rewind in subjecting camera
skewed evidence for which no home is found

~~durable quantum~~
however you see a past ornaments mode pond
doorway registers to enter outdo shuffles us

~~omit module emotion squares~~
some bitter taste for which no home parcels
out evidence or other afternoon pretonic levels

job trance flight horizon two-point turn options
a way to land in axis orbit rift halt pivot energy
~~moods us as~~

what you know in this field before the next
meeting tops off the cubicle direction theme
~~condition from~~

~~variable regression the point grid of~~
signs and numbers have we got anything right
edge sense gaming what odds to luck give way

more stuff to push off never gets enough tight
dig let go current snow foregrounds with what
~~did you do that for stop~~

loosen turf slam pallial speed triggers no
amount resides along bodies momenta transact

afternoon scripts right foot first
overcross to any open window day
lean pursues wandering themes far
enough beneath a surface to forget
what they who we are even quick
fingerpaintings make sense their
silent explosions approaching
though not yet familiar enhance
shorthand level float one and all
results following domain elliptic
slow down speed arrow ads that
anyone could claim as past visit
storage bins warp and slide surface
from elsewhere rough sport locus a

~~spell from the~~
~~characters of another alphabet~~
greenbuilt lunar month brood
piecemeal agrarian matters
whereon each hour of a day is
represented by shadows of a stilus
blunt point probe although anything
erodes with repetition paral-
lelograms reposition pelagic tables
any cylinder gnomon marked under
sun rain hail froth against red rock
cliff wind squall disorienting birds
cicada pipe stridulant ellipsis
frames the deck and sunshine from

labor down to organizing principals fade at the bitter again already to documentary photos conclusive unless foldbelts tend to braid as counterflux tends to plus without limit or white water tends to bottle as moraines tend to minus with no more pure than real image embroidered with arms penned wish conduit where fragrance expects to bring home not that excited about here impatient to get out so this or that bends to explain after particular eye view dynamite where some could touch the remodeled ceilings neoswing lyric signatures identify what she would say already said in expected retreats an incandescence runs through in complaints about any thing orchids cancelled by car honk at that crippled road runner ripple effect brings us all up to speed impatient equation parts and whole ghost hungry speech traffics ~~after swallow knock on wood hours~~

which to observe the equinox gnomon pillar as canon index for accurate dialing to know exactly how bright passes any given plane containing measurement identifies there when she thought herself included with that trained pear although of two minds voiced in the usual octave eliciting familiar twosomes along Numa arches to face east and west true false ancient coins depict *janua* passage how a rule of two results in the rational third given by number asunder dividing the day's ellipsis frame twined in step close step dance approximate beginnings as like as parallel fires although enough light let through for an observer at the back to see without being seen how velocity measures in counterflux braid fold belt crest moraine with reciprocal overpoems the topsails to remove or stockings that layer us a particular somewhere separate corresponds to

~~hold what is not in the mouth~~
slat-daubed cadence until something means
too long down to the minute boundaries rescue

and move out of debt affords different ways to
combine weight and shape key call numbers
~~punctuate~~

~~a lively print embalmed~~
views to be effective there before you some-
times no amount of labors toward the opposite

ritual long drive in red zone deadline stripped
the yet to be seen daily index for prelude ruins
~~the whole thing~~

laws for whom space outpost orchestrating
beat orders no vibrato her voice a soprano sax
~~holds the phrase~~

~~any day of the week~~
soft chair video deeps feel like fun we're no
worse off an afterlist dress for playful combat

just that meaning provides those closest to
arrange embrace functions in rebalance funnel
~~that office she is in elsewhere we recognize~~

how to make sense of it flowcharts whitewater
flood range knotted on string surrounding
~~tissue firewheel pulse button~~

THREE PM

check sheets cover bargain desert landscape
dust funnels   tandem birds balance pocketing air
we push forward with jackhammers and plastic pipe
shards reconfigure   now tense holds in purple glue
star heat spiked conduit

aquifer translates to mimosa scented shade
with *hic et nunc* in cloud cool almost rain
so many worlds pivot
killdeer   gillnet   button hook   proem
the *hematopoiesis* of bone marrow

saying natural world for example when what remains
revisionist frontier   seedbox   groundsel
between orange barricades workmen signal
road access   familiar routes brass beaten
air bowls to carry this electro mask buddha hour in hyperflame

what are you ready for
prepackaged cool wait for
rentals to happen left hand
skills demonstrate surprising
numbers survive with mental
health intact numbed after
disaster events lose the ability
to feel certain emotions don't
pursue homes with guns in
them wake up calls for it
remains to be seen let the
matter rest spelled out
messages from earth on gold-
plated records ninety minutes
of over sixty languages
diversify practical down-
home rootedness social fabric
changes overnight whistle
stop target audiences dread
longing to divide the climate
more americans on parole
distracted by this or that war
backyard burn barrels why
has this not been given
attention people should be
very worried downwind areas
rise ahead of curve rains
increase spread of disease the
web's sense of timelessness
behave according to codes of

Four PM

out of tango world sweep slide point context each line breathes
on gaphold transom snaps or too busy to attend to slips
circadian *infradian* *ultradian* rideout
already taking place with everything you respond to

blinds open and close toward what you might think as kite breeze at
equator velocity and other from the beginning
clockworks oscillating to habit a feeling traces
already takes place in everything you'll respond to

the way slow sun draws on a poppy despite some let fall
energy warp orbit moments taken in quiet to
restore dance grammars with dream catalog balance beam climb
where everything takes place already and you respond from

that trunk of an inclined tree drops to the ground shapes rule here
what arrests us later levels out in private entry
myth frame stream talk or black lake doldrum lull body traffic
you already place everything with responses taken

toward what you might think absent   verified points generate time   then choose vegetable
A positive   alright second comings now to fossil fuel   she is not how you feel   loud cling
rhythms from someone else's poem   where to get the best ones   what you cannot look
away from enunciates pouty and thick   put that energy into bagatelles letting go of flat

not just another nail clipping   duck in the row   unfinished being romantic drag   an agent
by synonym legend   colors his story without her points of view   food already prepared
rarely so easily as she wishes wisdoms   languid draw taxed out   doorglass   green *fica*
dustsheen mythic scents through your body   cell dial   how long holds onto   breath trail

high open april winds overstrung in sand breath   by clouds I am outrun   here in a fourth
month as though ends begin   run the kite with fireworks tail   give up on the   parallel
searches each our turn pulse pace level   photoburst   killboxes in colombine in kosovo
let go aftermath stunned list broil I however my own life to noise   glue mouthstrike waver

polyverse despite big-brimmed hats and sunglasses from texas being into brings the energy
scan boundaries between amid   strength becomes in the occasion   seeing it a second time
to what extent choice conditions   conditioned in correct content and dated black figures on
ashlight   if it feels like fun then   around gaps heart habits close   dream white page waked

a way to rebuild toward being shapes through ears rounded for
godglyphs by flowering waterclock and chaos *diel*
under light block flaxseed eye pillow doze sustains check out
where everything you respond to already has taken place

next to pitch a fit histories in what does it mean when
purple or gold events as entirely something else
places everything you respond to already taken
from forgotten catalogs which she cried about later

a moment taken life clock switch in fourth month lexicon hour
respond to everything that already takes place in you
tuned out from surrounding phase wind batter and late bud freeze
wake thoughts change reinventing habit stretch wheel as *plan A*

already taken places everything you respond to
distracted feelings family lifed could emigrate between
series of floor plans even solitude enacts like news
not telling a story but surviving in the sum of

Five PM

after *deja vu* ramp clog
pan flash record meteor hits
hidden events radiate present landscape
shop like crazy cleans context
early winter deliberates nuclear claim
drive through dinner red eat neon perhaps flashes empty transit slump spike like where to enter words meaning not you defines enough to get by crossroads motion the butterfly wing undertakes misheard as cannot be helped to provide the gap anyone can do though if I were someone else or a personal trainer before it disappears would ravel in tonight's cleanup day figures on shut that off piano series
getting to top breaks even
everyday crises mummify one bookkeeper
her mind music remains locked
different people hear the message
survey consensus after weeks polling
for you to see it according to how picks up on something else to work toward sometimes escape preface with let go of that also a full plate aubade for evening urban newsak section head in the song to cover barking dogs at closed out twilight mandorlas named for who knows which way to consider set up as undergrowth for operatic stars wrapped so bright *spica* sidelines *venus* and *mars* for *hydra leo virga*
buy and sell pieces of paper
over time exposure elements blink
not fair scorecards adjust order
argue further airbrushed romantic circles
europa's water supply made plural
ideally folds would not appear to have equal weight however something must remain behind along peripheral banners treadmilled for you as part time measures the *into void* some winds duning higher than others and rearrange by file almost impossible to nonsense where relaxed and open around straight lines those fast foods floor dance as though certain steps occur to us in a first place recognizing
perfect picture mission picks battle
underfunding's dark zipcode attacks present
bilateral symmetry axis spotted there
introductory offers free fall erosion
sky blue oil pools testify

one hand then another out of into the hammock under a gazebo if you can fund repair work for short roof beams and ruined wood coming from anywhere to smooth stop gap tangle sounds we stand at a window somewhere to leap understands the need for solitary flight after make you feel good or bad choice roads move across inspecting for trickle through meanings as if pillars appear there

female paradigm impersonates replacement therapy
trick phrases play the mouthpiece
scramble for crumbs accounts for
given time do more work
lucky dog spots street life

become the messenger fails to identify pregnant places between violin and cello forget misease magnetic flux-fields around the head resonate with tight gloves close your eyes efficiency bead count smooths repeat words shape to hear one after another mooring right now the only place to check on who you are perfectly cool beside the last implosion designed to clear away old bridge posts that cannot adapt

shadows show phil stays out
arsenal explodes yo-yo string tangle
point a revolver buys valentine
we help you change crescendos
how scar tissue fits in

to faster vibrations keep at it thresholds groove until eke out writes in as landslide even shallows move faster like anything I never keep up with centers pick and choose from too little to say except those observations anyone could have made before tonight's sun setting and me not ready to limp over the edge into no gods know which war *ethnically clean* inside out upside down takes time to consider

false self too much alike
cheaper than direct graffiti painting
answers occur half asleep milieu
make my kick butt day
whole cities pout and whine

don't ask just drive indulges in whatever comes to mind steal a sense of the world continues to unravel gray with no more teeth in the comb for spinning and sore limbs unwilling to take flight at appropriate moments we guess at no longer grateful for crux of the situation and other constant motions that tire me when I look in the mirror not reassuring a source of concern for how will assemble all the help hired for a style to which I accustom myself although no one is watching yet

after war there's nothing wrong
children reflect painted over economy
prepare for make do rumors
lives a product for *mcjobs*
mind change channel busters click

as we always think someone must these days where I curl up and let bliss file terror
abandoned we get used to anything except a stone in the shoe forces to march until
lunch time or is it supper where they look the same if you stretch your arms and
squint one eye shut adjusted hues merging an overall design or let it happen the
way a glass elevator already in place tumbles down toward me anyway the right
image for an hour's meditation so as not to drift further into nothing made out from
divide up your whole self
mottled trees line the road
a bee reason rushes up on
yin-yang paradigm shift flood market
superwoman works out in home
doing what I want while no one forces me to stay here wobbles in a pattern I
maintain pinning myself so I comply just right the way a little wire touches the
battery to keeps things basic what possesses you sometimes obsessing on how the
words take us along to catalogue anywhere I look predisposed by urban nature
offramps and the particular instruments of measure we use to engulf or move out
from overarching tumbler styles into volcano quaketide thermospheres mine strung
comfort culture skate unions fall
sword gambit trauma junkies militate
as art your life material
our feet virtually in anything
my shadow looking at hers

Six PM

to eat while watching the news we
browse along shuddering footholds
skipped rip-rap *newsak* moves on to
miami's aging overweight & serial killer, how he
shoots himself   disappointed by future downloads

disappointing the FBI   overarmed   overeager
as excusework we separate to
draw in lines for driveby   for commodity stalkers
unable to surf the perfect wave   ooo-ah-ommm
toward opportunity shores unshadowed

into fog bowed weather we climb
through yesterday thinking & too much caffeine
ramble where all I am connects
across glass-break profiles
we leave out   slide anchor in the bright white effable

rob the bank next door to
keep your numbers up
supplement income with
other jobs build revenue for
kids in college know the
business inside and out
undergoing rapid change
builds a career on atmosphere
maybe there are witch hunts
launch an investigation of
ways to say change or die
survivors camp in the street
pump disinfectant no hope of
rescuing anybody flip
channels crumpled bodies
newly homeless string tents
shift focus from denial forum
dead hand built in on nuclear
warheads try to out think
destructive mentality 50
years in advance maintain
anxiety around nothing
polarize issues take with you
more than you leave a
complicated bargain though
meaning was never clear in
the first place shrink public
radar screen fresh *newsak*
sandia watermelon bomb and
missile depot stockpile topoff

SEVEN PM

electric wire lift-off rims

white cosmos garden dial

jupiter to the right of

october's inflated moon

recension pulls pocked white slate

bright overhead night blaze blues

this continuum’s moment

gold cirrus hedge shadow coal

pearl virga brush gap slant set

mindful ebb   ,bound summit draw

scan and sift rivet path spin

urban pack surface shift

west branch blood pulse flutters bent

crest switch tram slides light litter

from east angle stars blink on

route 66 slowride flood:

french quarter then mesa pawn

discount food mall burgers tires

touchfree carwash budgetel inn

modular tumbleweed inc

clearance center lounge cluster

vacant site R V palisade

four by four jeep ride home camp

blockbuster clip string shot curve

hand sign gift shop stone bag walk

tissued theme graffiti track

albuquerque fractal sprawl

toward teen lined rap car street quake

stage whistle pocket smoke lit

dog tag brass fired glass raze cool

impersonate dead surf swarm

duskmata smudge fields echo

car beam guide streak red or white

hat backwards   ,frost wind leg whips

kick burst park lamp side aura

voice gong flood seeps off side

testimony mouth sweep lure

translate goatspur   ,red thistle

ash tent moths leaf bite drop

home road stoop straight on cloud catch

sky cello neck scarf dust kiss

abobe clay baled niche curve

carved cottonwood dance rattle

native art   ,entropy fenced

mesa fire rabbit road crush

east park bluegrass fountain swoop

apple orchard gray lace tuft

choice shadows firework ,shutter

ember tree reach sway fades out

dust kites lie down ,pause breathes in

walk narrowing to night jar

dusk bird poor will outline call

barred flashwings flutter span from

bare ground nest house pads devour

water panned axis blade ,lead

sharp edge sand text weighs deeper

knee foot chill fog path shawl slope

chitalpa blossom clots glow

on night's curb we arrange with

corn maze ticket exit hall

nature collar chain outdoors

black bear wolf coyote hawk

cut short animal mask view

steel flags tank ,sectored sky bent

hair on end thirst mesa stands

pueblo shoulder slope rose turn

wall rug woof hung mud straw pose

feel of dream horse mane guitar

oil pot pastel mountain grid

dense miss a beat island stretch

inside cactus breath needles

arroyo upturn dry chokes

granite bank gneissose tempered

I circle   browse   spark hungry

ruined beauty's concrete ladder

drainpipe boxed run-off swirls clear

ash   ,slag layers   silt settled

windborne scuff cowl frame stave where

no one builds we climb reaching

Eight PM

plastic bags white flag prairie sage

electric wire fence clouds leap ,coast

sequin foothill mountains walk me

here buck rabbits freeze ,gaunt in

slow turn eye fix asphalt heat shrill

on streams of air an insect wing builds up draws forward in figure eights an experimental animal where flight muscles attach to a thoracic box which acts as a spring found most attractive where observed rhythmic features of song provide progress and isolation in a series of different acts once thought to intend the beeswax honey or bite

herself a random unit leading up to past events she considers how to describe a mechanism or leap an instant collected in time distinctly until sequence fades in and out depending on particles observed while motion continues to the right to the left whited out at intervals where zones present themselves to be bombarded according to simpler

barks, bird call, bead count, gravel rings

the traffic lit moons puddle skip

acequia spill red ,oil streaks

a packed horizon scrawls cross lace

stranded with pocket pager I

move on ,hand to foot in thought pulled

midge swarm over decorative carnivore lives add on to all we've seen sorting through history check and go afterprojects wild for a fee short storm winkout rifts locate on your standard swing phrase episode level every day run of the mill climates groove into milestone flukes or lightyears at different speeds the voice rises through main

refracting radio signals imply how to bend and slow according to structure like tin cans or gourds under wooden bars pitch mellow where padded mallets strike according to photos with other data still heading up from a plane for this duststorm blanket crossing rills canyons and wrinkled skin though sun heat falls at a comfortable slant

flower tree branch spring blown dust zones

then monsoon tempered sun stretches

straight up ,slide westerly leaf drops

coined fire from blue plate sky ,mares tails

sweep ,turn coat collar up against

night's thick plumage scar erasures

combine solid fuel rockets for missile propulsion with being for example a nervous gray matter cerebrum cerebellum the blood-hound the lockheed igniting in air after supersonic speeds a stovepipe in flight though temperatures will be higher and unable to start from rest connectors leeward easily as nettles to soft fiber land fill jettison

classical practice diagrams a move away from certain sentiments common to a spectrum of approach ambiguity sweeps through aimed toward more varied and relaxed as handbooks on pleasure array to celebrate eventual release without pinpoints special days occur for an ordinary person the thing itself images in dance food music incense the play dissolves receiving

this cul de sac's torn box spring scape

where bent streetlight buzzed nature stares

moth caught ,transparent wrap flickers

NINE PM

for Jan Heide
(1947 - 1998)

expand narrow attention
alien floors hold
life praxis
tomorrow repetitions

a woman paces at the overhead screen
          words don't cook rice

begin with your name
to hold the shade in place
tap shout words cook rice perhaps as
five checks point a scene
between us reassemblance

it feels like to go there becomes what is in front of you

though you might imagine   ,get busy
insists upon reawakening
means take us   before deep swim explores in

their *there*
               as well as your *here*

I don't remember how you see it
                                        where make do nests fly from

troubled sleep transforms
          while a deceptive lull

hairline beauty wisps her described edge

          breath gulp   fragile waver puzzle
          word acts love   so either or
vision spokes uptake   referents she speaks in

flight after so much weight loss though veins plump you up with fluids

one person's edge tool
          in laughter practice

          insufficient reminds us of nearby
also confusions a sentence requires

deflects challenge
          until calm untroubles   ,rest harrow
maps toward country to be set out

energy shapes the way her eye sees along a breathpath where you are vision projecting these fear points that concentrate ego for comfort like this bright red shirt worn signals to protect footprint and temperature transmuting how you are here looks out as an extroversion separating you from in between which no longer applies to an island frame or fluttercore hold on conventional wisdoms the elegant wallpaper might arrange as you

or someone you know so what is the use of such a wound to hold until it closes pure donkey willow leaf incense attachment strike curve divagation a pervading circle whirled loose from its mooring and over the white fence paling toward tie it off retrieval repetition into wished for clarities we go by moving left to right then upward from down and across in order not to build a house at random bound under logic of water and empty light

where simple satisfactory corners beacon strafe through goal post banners in startling yellow caught helioabyss drop day ground breath knocks here in a shriek like peacock gatekeepers until out there forms the void of you to recognize precipitates as that no longer between everything places where we agree a bed might be raised lowered with flowers nearby without shaking your attention in shrike quaver ululu across your shoulder

turn under ash salvage folds from bluegreen border haze moment wherever carries gulp the air craving oxygen though cells refuse and let go to quasistellar animal flight fog love holds let go even touching hands will not describe moon capped water dried into figuring space panics that questions carry and tie here a way we please one another will no longer necessary the sequence of signs from urn dressed night   from throatcenter

life kiss word litter plumbline drop
rudder drift music turns under
cut-pattern day for
growth reliquary   bone case
to continue without confusion
each hour begins and ends
foraging wherever chaos is undertaken
all of it real world
jewel bones radiate

a way the future shapes us needing somewhere to go and we will do for now basket shape in rock range we adjust to sharpened limits from can and cannot returning to unthinkable a place it had been so you stay with me as internal property: a *clinamen* though not exact childhood or harp curve approximate but bridgey i am yours as another where we come to inhabit distance by echolocation that faultless and clear arranges itself from so far away you are how you do it rescored mosaic drone gamut number properties explain space for you are as boundary shifts across which breath draws under something known

you are space between me   beetle wing flutter and door
back rock   lion practice   posture clasp
from a wish to be cared for   ,the caretaker
arms circle repeating
to loosen the drawn nerves
upper body held as though hollow
knee flex motion
lifts the feet from the ground
solid transom attitude burst

come back with flowering willow herbs
do not clip the curl from your fine red hair
for shelter arranging points on white light
a gate drag where you are
water poured into water if you ask what is the use of
push pull cloudlit ellipse in so much
dream grid wish ties at the left shoulder
a corner of the mind rests
through variegated names to hold us

before between breathhold to mark which numbers
progress along a charcoal line

hemp link   whale net   blue directions

punctuate a way to herd emptiness with
parallel vibrations the means to travel whatever can be connected

not collapsed into
certain attractions shape the throat's eye

cello upcurve though precipice until a child sings
clean   held high a moment above obstacles   hair crossline

how to treat separates into leave behind
and thinking so spaces

what we ask for and other panoramas
doorframed   gap hover   wrath piece

as though certain steps off
standing struggle limb balance

collide appropriates with melodic detail
for example, how heavy you feel in water

as thirsty cells grow careless
peripheral slide tones quaver in the voice

anything pleasures given a stage to circle
specifics let go   frostboil   energy hollows

like the hook of a cool north route without sidetracks
or emotion at the speed of sound *through variegated names to hold us*
a corner of the mind rests
notion engages background *dream grid wish ties at the left shoulder*
accords a style for gesture then shakiness returns *push pull cloudlit ellipse in so much*
water poured into water if you ask what is the use of
like a short vertical line to repeat what you were saying *a gate drag where you are*
may or may not reveal an end point further on *as shelter arranging points on white light*
do not clip the curl from your fine red hair
come back with flowering willow herbs

maps toward country to be set out

until calm untroubles ,rest-harrow
deflects challenge

also confusion a sentence requires
insufficient reminds us of nearby

in laughter practice
one person's edge tool

flight after so much weight loss though veins plump you up with fluids

vision spokes uptake referents she speaks in
word acts love so either or
breath gulp fragile waver puzzle

hairline beauty wisps her described edge

still a deceptive lull
troubled sleep transforms

where make do nests fly from
I don't remember how you see it

as well as your *here*
their *there*

means take us   before deep swim explores in
insists upon reawakening
though you might imagine   ,get busy

it feels like to go there becomes what is in front of you

between us reassemblance
five checks point a scene
tap shout words cook rice perhaps as
to hold the shade in place
begin with your name

        words don't cook rice
a woman paces at the overhead screen

tomorrow repetitions
life praxis
alien floors hold
expand narrow attention

Ten PM

nights out
egress then ,ravening
cool fall escort
brake forward shift sparring to wake
nerve surf ,stay up
yes no petal quilt scatter
notion bind
joy negating sleep
perpetual mind change queries
whose nightly
twilit transit
movie where choirs sing each other
through name drenched sunset blades
carrying foot tremulous
dawn for one more unruined stage
or let me not injure
simple focused
a way night heron stalk the gulf
life plans written on a napkin at jack's bar
one year ,five years
keep waking
relations tissue methodical ,befuddling
filter gate

narrowing dusktide gaze
even tepidarium
string lit night boat
wine glass halved
temperature of silence
inferred by cricket register
unheard rhythms a surrounding
no longer to finish everything else first fashions
opening wedge
period instruments devise
flittering buff gray low flight dead leaf
tongues cut to please across the ear
twilit closure
yes hears in *every word is so deep*
dark red bumping along the ground to
alternate rope works
by which we transit undertow
invisible afterspill
where letters describe
I recognize you
this is all we have
I feel you growling outside my window
I trace you dancing behind the slur of
tree branch white slate pocked
flashing tips of your fingers to
balance fleshing cold stars
into a river we re-enter
test bEEp-bEEp-bEEp erasures
memory's day slant attar

remains manage
at least public selvings
float tether sandbag jettison imaginals
beside a white fire city
ordinal whatever pendings
late downturn
albatross shock portions
unknowable *the* meditations
scenario rustblack imaginary
for a while skein by skein
loss collapse

a means toward sleep on night runways
cleared to fringe spark cliche
in kick the wolf from the door chant
still at work through sequence direction requires
transition maps the body
survive death's rehearsal
play dead
like monday's teton jogger
attacked by endangered bears
freeze in time
until coma vigil climbs onto
air view flow charting
how to clarify outside discussion
commands ,cries for help
fresh views point us
omitting speech latitudes
no longer human

expanding vacancy neon decor unfolds dissemblance queen of heart smoke though healing faster than expected gifts once given demand from now on reviewed and counting what she has more reflective this attention to absence to aversions of the eye the face the mouth except wild about your list of how to think about breath while speaking works for a while mood paralysis in high in low wheeled replacement breathes deeply listening all we are given this life to practice a focusing made to fill the blanks determined by

imitating
thought
air gulps
in out of state landscape
whine vortex
negative energy solo
gives life to except
laughing ,relaxing then trigger strike
shapely though thin and curious remain
nameless music hums

shadow lit dance accountings palpate
a way we step across
each space to fill ,ephemeris log
scratch and scribble thread polygraphies
where high desert light sprawls unprevented
nature's counterclaim
until detector blazed ground cover all night long
if anything moves
nocturnous ,noctuary
unreal night joggers circle gold lamp streets
consider every antonym for salt drafts a means to
let go in evening edge banter
touching down from dusk interval
surf drum recessionals do not interfere

journal rip-rapped door stalk
exact chaos station
afterday repetitions chant

vine deformation rift transport flash
after grocery pick-up
drives east into

live color polemic introducing beyond along with decorative context particulars in speech poster rumors nobody there anymore tradition breaks in on to try remembering as you describe mined jewel contours ready to give up everything each time chainsmoking pounds the details into some universe retrieval swarm despite miles away from epicentered reconstructions those new *killer stars* streak toward
a fresh set of proofs
confusion
wavetable
timbral aggregate night channels
a wash of collected objects lift ,pop ,tap
intrasonic routines

august nights pare to perfect respite rasp
she wants this unportioned
the past making its way through
accepted meanings
because tells her and
often too early to draw a line through
capable adjusts into should
therefore simply this life
this day's means to contain war

on a scale of one to ten where choice surfaces what slope changes your dialogue plane together under anvil strike skies and other deadhand ambush we build to inherit us for a last hurrah fictive fetishing squalid speech drape days violence varies in harness rub and chafe removal forgotten watching one another for tally mark slash the usual bitter encasements left behind if time permits where shorthand meanings not quite what we plan sometimes acronym a crossing void impellent air currents balm in body scent where the phoneme happens is important as
quotidian harp whether we listen or
interrupters pulse response
an energy to stay out of sync

float through winter seasons tour lit
from flat-hulled gray white galleons
above occasional ground-drawn lakes at carlsbad
fishing long dark piers
storm chain skies fluoresce

fireant pitch case striving

vespered straphang

you filter

vortexed life what you give to

usual sough siffle wind company

ghost courtesans

only those who return are rewarded

close look no one turns out

romanced memories connect us in
impatient to get to the point
as if applies
mostly represented with
not quite here
if it works issue perimeters
nowhere's chaos flesh hemmed
distinct darkness to
compete with nature
high yield temperatures
bakery harvest of

pounding on detail until a universe appears

to be like

fear praise zodiac side-reels

what happens break span

inner scatter

leisure momento scew

looking close in on describe

the into downwork

blood and oxygen understand

comfort abrasions grey slide link

gambist terrain pluck

impletion rigor

sleep hedge pneumatic

heart beat voice overs in the only sounds we know

version as who you are

with other simple goals

floor dancer phrased

center stile palm lever

lost at how to identify that premise

image points adapt along the

phase in phase out

halfway there's
selective country
not the person
I knew then
when invents
reinstall suspicion in
good as it gets
which way up strategy
she finds herself repeating
any guess mad border
by way of explanation
same way solve
going for hope thinks
too hard listening
lost interprets longer
to from premise
electronic ocean skies
the necessary luxuries
never doors we waver at

deserting long unpaginated labor
shapes also view in
ice whisper
served-up shadow flotation
to might as well the endings
cover the yard finch cage
anechoic pillowing rush pulse
inner voice perch diagonal crossing
blueblack bridgesway star wink
read each other recurring in
what's already there possibility crux
dimmed peripheral vision along paper ephemera
forever captures in spherelike trajectory

urban nebulae
night sky culminates in
quick shadow flight burst
and car window hammer music
screen flash war shuffle
we've stretched the ozone gulf to more than
twice the size of Europe
another occurrence delivers to
dusk edge rattle
collective margins define
recycle bare barbed voices
unlace obsession sculpting sleep where
anyone whose energy touches you
afterimages through dark letter shore page
washing upward in
sandhill crane echo field curved closer
together sleep wreathes us in
the way alone

ELEVEN PM

for JG

and hours fill with themselves
waiting impatient for more attention
logos asleep under notched pages and the pencil
beside my pillow   reach left after
dream fog tensions erupt   day erasures

if unattended
weeds leggy and sparse
each point a story we make by looking further into
arrival   driving away   composite walked notes
tried   discarded   to incubate quiet closure

under a cobalt mirror even the sungod closes her eye
at least once every 29 days   I leave the notebook
to stay asleep
logos nods   each angle guessworks
into night reef shape   mooring tomorrow's windward

mountains of trash antibiotic
cocktails einstein's theory of
relativity explained in less
than nine minutes we've
made big conceptual moves
lately there's nowhere to be
but on collective attention
span portable street bubbles
fly all over crawl under the
table wallow in history chunk
one between subtle shading
and the absence of light lies
just to give you a sense of
scale over time a pygmalion
for everyone heading home
from vacation computer
apartheid even mobile homes
become missiles reach
another level then let go
make it to the top of the list
in time to live conserve
animals bedlam theater focus
too much on private lives
complaints filed as a matter
of policy no one says it's
working perfectly the power
to make her own life separate
good with numbers it's not
clear what they're deciding
even chickens won't drink the
water the question is whether
or not it's appropriate strong
nerves needed the sum of
transplanted parts eight hours
of tape edited to one perfect
minute if you're not going to
be despairing a pot of blue
paint stains the skylight fills
the chasm in debate silence
not hard to understand make
up frontier look for survivors
in seeing and hearing isn't
always believing call it a
memoir a toxic tour of the
city soaks up pretend it won't

MIDNIGHT

reeds along the sea ruff ,whiter as night proceeds translate ,or travel by blight
my piecework ox and me

past the heart stop
simplicity of I ,ear mark

eve enters pandora vortex

as though nominal ascent imagines
fixed for a moment details of

overcoming shock in
hands on slap and shake other(ings

sand color serious break down limo
an I through life
change operates the inside handle
which opens from the outside here
panic handle then to get through the next layer

site events tear in order to say
freedom ,scaled and stratified

seeing a line through her I
through my I

as in *she has performed her personality all afternoon* ,then intermittent
agrees to say this ,or

who knows march steps the possible un)masks
where occurrence amounts to something you can trust
a vocation to sort the grain from mood harness

and besides ,who can be pleased
media fragged
desiring then ways to manage

along ice riddle conscience

there is music for travel as in

how long expectations follow the schedule holidays timed keep

a culture live stays in you define outburst portable Ives example from now poet rap

pop pop pop

the phone in another room
target for whose question this is
a decided matter

understand as fiction

thinking what to do

to take up as though river drag extracts yield

toss and turn rhythms leap in leap out void for how many ways can you have it list grows by someone's outreach bus run through heartcastled air we breathe confront matters gruel affect with connect-the-rose futures choosing real term acts and blind echo lines in justified seven-eight notation gorged by truck jams expanding a neighborhood tack wish story for whose escape solution arriving at chance moments in your automatic is different from mine surprised historicities fire

apnea

understand it all transitions
the exile of is
the thing itself leaves behind

hallucinations verified
abecederium

wherein the text places her
chrysalis perimeter
flaw statue
dreamatic marble
vernal equinox moment

men of words admire men of words listen

not surfing but drowning ,shelf drop opens

do you think you enjoyed it
at the time or was it later
to follow faster on the expensive heels of America

abbreviate reflect as strange territory

how each link flares to save by repetition and avoidance keep it long enough to forget you have it uniforms locution intervene siren flag for this person center seen distance in contact with tree sprout struggles for a front row seat along with other displaced bedlam each moment's reincarnate feeding station replete with next day watch the team win as I win vagabond smoke nothing to show for gabbler's ulysses and sister sun everywhere hum behind the heart continents media packages wrap once we say it moving on to although stories amazed with civil hedgerows of privet events while other questions in degree we follow one another not sure the premise speaking will get to where and added to be motions patterned for chipping toward mistfeed migrant closure we identify as one another stasis points coming in at where you are I am struck

across white shore echo gauntlet
absence expects us through

schemata ,shadowframe too late she recognizes

moth bright flutter
counters
depend upon

newscast dream wake

chilean grape orbit shrink
for closed eyelids

to color just so

To practice flame, preparation imagines the point of entry. Night's dusk holograph erased by stars. Intervene quiet. Need backslides thin branched in revised moorings flutter vein re-entry gap. At last she happens water frame where habit sketch spits you out. Opposition might according though often not. Glissando casts between teeth and lips. Allow a hold. Response shore flight red white rudderings. Give me up. Intend perhaps revels in soft context alarm errant necessity rathers. Lip sync beat axis mediates. Hunger measure. Perfectly devised bramble thick and mellifluous. Sometimes she thinks meadow in snare fiber seeding the mirror. Curtain blown referent flood outside someone intersects as shelter. Sand metronomes curve shift, revealing more as islands ascend to choose their attention. Downdrift calls completion. Sustaining most of the body. Sound lumen escape range resigns into afterimage wanting to cover evenly. This twilight cannot reoriginate, though there are marks for leaving. Less colorful later and select coordinates. You can't always be. Leave messages although the clear circuit quietly mistakes being centered a little to the left of confused night bay. According to old patterns. Listen for. Runway flash, whatever air provides a tool. Hour sketch notions.

reflected ,steers

like a life she encounters

layer praxis mine swallow details

a drive for profit lets go

she tells me she will also
extend might assumptions toward endure
okay then ,contagion's red apple drenched in bee's wax
for deep breath ticklish coughs
help me orient my self
battle coarse healing
seizure ,compromise

more sound cusps too far out

relic dress recourse writes us out an although whip for angry weathers ,nature walk in traces
through no nature to fear except where fault chaos effects the
can we kill everything narration its coherence as though one voice in
dialogue time catches where *single text terrorists* throw bricks at center scatter

typing on a billboard
in desperate match obliterating dreams
study maps where I am not here

format slams bolt somewhere
to make each letter love
with compulsive *ghazals* of childhood

despite
in the beginning she resists ,not quite how the word scalpel resides in a
need to mean scalpel , *scalpellum* even before the 16th century a small, light knife

dispassionate
despite severe service undertaken
how rainfall slant of 80 degrees means wind speed algebra scores
let go above a branch strewn pool
life forces its way
between this day and tomorrow's cardboard plutonium box

One AM

how to thrive world mirror talks a night hour's
second language dambreak bright continua
though we pretend it is not plane circled light
one red also the bark of the sumac or willows
cat's eye and mews for someone who trains in
a right direction to put others out he wants us
all to herself struggle choose my once beast of
legs hair shower me putting the basis decide
want that programs transit immune effect in
you have to be places hospitaled months pass
karma immaculate beside this drink what is
practical ease lie present dutiful vacant here
not even particulars follow a person to be as
herself at the time feeling obverse invisible
shines other meaning that's so rhythm owed
known compels us alone from nursely glaze
dispenser swallowing goddess the gods will
swallow fast growing sails people around in
a good river taken to levelled best outcome
side effect in pelvic bone staged numbs the
marrow needle despite fresh airs with next
door soul radio yes the body does this for you
this rest midstream challenge drawn bigger
tracks forest zone as hummingbird moment
patient in sea salted water retable wavers

Two AM

childhood remembers the facile garden page driven
toward what prism flare the woman's etude marking
white water dreams us differing screen arc surfaces
glow loud energy expands where requisite givens fit
who she is not who she is next time these undertake us
from blue silk transmuted each day's memory large
enough to yesterday shade fragrance triage driven a
way of sorting work life speaks to wake in shapesift
memorized self mood swung a nightbook edge song
in)complete opening to more than bird walks remain
overfed a shelf staged watchful if you're having any
problem theatre under the influence breaks into what
ever we say perhaps as the dead in a series of stations
geographies arranged by color one finds let's say as
too much red the eye draws in while not yet like our
yellow storm light entering toward turn from later or
until new bed soft slept on amazements choose a way
to tell some story we rest through awe carried further
to become our next clarity white water screens with
prelude and september junk rumor swept full boxes
where high cool walk from dinner's road I step back
and forth pull(ed under cloud brush heat flashed sky
toward autumn call to hear vowel rung cone flower
crosshairs at which we find ourselves voice mirage
clipboard or hovercraft breathe deeply paths draw on

Three AM

as hearing wavers warp absence in doubt gliding cloud
ether conduit mast caught by hand circumference to
aurora tagged past a desire inkwelled beauty rains
darkening window dust fresh siffle one floats on
where cutleaf drops the heady sunflower stem

little red magnetic poles us accounting for an
I content daily into this week next arrives at
summer listing upon safe seamed lives we
legwork unerotic fooled first cricket chirp
as fan motion rib lights litter wall scratch

bruised turnings on left shoulder electron
exit site burn tissue salt mix potato salad
so simple even a judge understands the
case unleashing sunday late sleep table
news tight bridge to where lovers leave

a pagoda series like job gruel health cared
ourselves alone spoken out of seconds too
late hunger only reason timid plate drag us
inert upward turn fierce norm burst fountain
taking fire licks the sweat from another event

entertainment snow bowled tantrum drive gain
stark woman metronome pulse windskirting silt
impossible scan range we place yield crash wave
overcurrent sweep flight due purpose reeling under
again turns beast lurch century off-street choirs lean in

Four AM

I shaped in the way you perhaps a country of moods lit
to become intended while trying to more simply again
dream begins without end not ending compare me the
shatter slept shadows followed upon ask appear then
reappear continuing new O rings we quark to carry
as refolded output we choose to explain ourselves
through choice handed off too quickly a rag wise
loop for clarity tracks us ridge after skin bridge
places here time to consider two strands I hold
separating to three as braiding rescues toward
any case shut down into dogged reactions con-
sider to what extent sprawl or punctuate tools
hitch ride im)possible frames we sail winded
watch for and not lifts flowing to mean what
could happen next or old song bright enough
to do the trick edge held in melodies wash up
on shore which way to turn arrangement curve
toward scat rung rest phrase a threshold crosses
in looking for something with the color an eclipse
dust depends on each one its own filter of distance
point string atmosphere flash ready I call from wave
what is the fog about treads water pinned fully though
seen through omitting layers quoted according to proofs
checked out serve it piping hot a trail cut shelter we figure
outposts here or there imagine curled under maculate veiling

Five AM

first letter reach again dust music ,wake tocsin blue swing consort in dust harvest curve a cabinet ,a piece of light to bear the life of the letter z as if examples z day to imagine the history of light ,no moment without its marred flare signal seen from tree lined rain lake shores meaning rivers then conversant ritual print and the way she carries mirror fragments the faces nod and shake their heads the I begins to recognize herself aphonic seasons turn ,squint ,grousing in how the I reflects back disappearing along a right edge like any word into history's light ,death citizen ,winked lightning ,gods' leashed breath practice log toward this world cafe to draw back upon sit up shout good morning serving line for number 00 only bank cards accepted ,but first z's day where I forget again what it wants to tell me at the anchor bolt of grief's door to whatever joy will mean

Six AM

spin through rebound weather the sanity of when in December's long styx
oasis I sleep in your arms through no greenyard blooms shaped in lucid
sound draws out to monkshood opening habit flowers cast alongside
familiar nervous energies a day truck wheels reduced for threshold unity

to intend lived I against rosing piqued glass vegetal and sand wedge
avenues which occupy bright hunger's name sung as third person then
calling it immemorial a story of other with fondness for the moment a
beach of one's own hands caught by attention of X or equivalent bodies

meaning changes how to talk about shares like other plecebo possessed
effects under a caped moon NE Saturn where *Fenris* tracks the world's egg
hung in the cloud-clawed furnace September swallows remember this
moving toward Wednesday not today stop waiting here as cold air extends

refuse to drink the red that waits here wasp at the throat where I think if I
heal and kiss the sun a slight headache system evidences marked tiers of
beech leaf then the laurel chosen by her name is laurel and how to deflect
a garnet undergone after ladders of blood and solitude between fine black

lines though not the nuclear waste room we bury under a slurry of salt in the cross stitch of consciousness a folded life resource seized by returning indecision to climb the mountain a ruined planet beauties autumnal light here as opposed to other cushions placed safe isolation body shut down

to undergo something done coordinates as another set of elevators and past the donor room where fresh collection gestures believe in singularity who do you think you are holding onto as seven words or less the steps retrieve in tick tock tick being fragments drunk from your mouth this I

SEVEN AM

wake chest hour transit slides the trumpet vine stretch skyward
medusa yawns   laze deep shadow choirs tune   breath whisper

prism seal zone for day labors flash blaze   do you cry   I don't
remember   crab claw pinch neck blood sweep circle hose

not black stockings but cell harvest if courage is no object if
why not a letter to say I love you only you and

you also a(lone   scrambled chance work   ,it is all our green stripe
image fills with a bray of mules boarded along the thick

alfalfa plot next door   do you cry   I didn't
wash the windows   get a job   crow signal clarifies the mesa

to learn a level of beauty read: wing bay   air letter
eye feather   ribbed specula   window dimmed sun glares

dog collar tag series prime steel tools   world wobble map pin
where I cannot embark in smooth phrase loop rush mention

experience depends more slowly from after words
washboard drive motion bolt rattle meditations on cause   here sequels differ

words overuse or strike to see objects toward how I describe you
lost sometimes how you describe me   exit index unfilled merges into

don't scatter   task mirage pulled from the belt of Nyx
accounts go about their business   twofold Lethe hand tracks

collect far enough to measure invention as we know describes
this is real when perhaps reaches for escape arms   ,fact after fact

needs list on use imprisoned for which case hang on
memory visions build   occasion a river of sunflowers beech leafed

discards winnow ocean drunk   taste the wake in
waiting's breath chamber   hinge   ,bowspring high and loud backlit

whatever we are used to placebo works   a storm shield
here and now underpoems   tread water   ice slip   draft ellipse

et al perceptions rebuild kairos cage kronos drag
time in time out contains the photograph   her color is good

the *vergiliae* call   skyboat years far away painted over
thrall barrow to navigate recitations for may   ,for november

morning struck flags nail down what is sky across the sun
scissored in from foghorse rider   shorter more opaque regenesis schedules

chakra climb to heat pierce   amulets tattooed in
coffee lute string space walk from diatonic rope rest

not even faults complete how this places the motion rose
what horizon polemics postpone tinge scarlet nimbus sponge

dialectic otherhands westward   triangle zigzag a natural tack with
polyvinyl bag as hill world razors flay under dimming Pleiads   ,name one

I know you are in there residues alert moments pure erasure
Neith heads up water tread over what would make good   shovel flash tools

day perfects resolution unless I drop the mirror in
reactionary happiness   the setting for name leaves out

insist on yet   never enough sections to except where sifting
without refraction umbrella   cinchweed break dries in eye shine

border flux   ,taut desire catalogs fluid mass view
tape secures the overlay   portal guides flow away at grill

I never got sick the whole time I was ill she tells me and
it is true here   facts chip-in to open door number five

if you choose means the amniotic river   ,threefold air
your hair trim bright with vocabularies of self invention

chain for suggestion yet other endings claim us
life   ,speech measures as though it knows

what it knows   ,rack witness perhaps graphed second(arily
a constellation of icons unreasonable collides

exquisite price echoes shore   white blank(et any more wilderness

EIGHT AM

to enter
exit the atrium
a means of closing questions
in overeaten pipe lined universe
untenable laps we knead we nourish
cue card *abecedaria*
the spatial orients who dictates as in
some people mode for this
where difficulties require toward
be there safe screen interpose
sift net shred
to punctuate survival no referent holds forth
though industry assumes ascent slope corner
history's tacit breath bate attributes
talk passing over one another through
yellow bulb embankments in beaten black dog night
chewed up dialogue's conducting shoal
where gild spin knots lose touch
with you are here ravel meanings to
heighten the label on
half world cut horizon horizons
intersect investment data effect
untouched by the natural wake station
a face brushing its teeth
turn from the gates
harness furrow

demand symmetries a little toward you've got it cusp
then breaks constant along our why matters
bigger suns than we see shown detail
curvature can be infinite not local
inference etching only etudes
intuit when this is reeled time
triple string harp strike anamnesis
day practice to signify or execute
written through the no one facets in myself or your
cyberhouse crossport shift edge
launch point relief sequence
our tenancy assembles war foraged
hyperbole stasis bloom heavenweed switch plate
click tokens power sweep the orient of space
re)clear bracework to how level
keep out zones gender engine mystery dress
operate the watch me watch me swim vortex
surrender preface to accept completion
hanging around at a beginning world view(ed
wishful thinking as given and due bright happiness
shout *hey hey are you okay*
colonize along someone's text bodies
time one uses to intervene or determine
formula compiled cricket equation vectors where
spoked instructions underline the what you know

water's nourishment
pours from the glass
handsful to carry morning deck glut
clutter by quaint angles leading its own
life a current pristine meadow where
I underline the speaking instructions
a fabulous hyperbole for motion shape
climbs inside the microphone
treadmill america island croons as
a girl might enter her public child
anchored in overpumped brackish water
to put someone together
listening for her own colorwheel
from prepared food junk assemblage
hunched barrier world sift chords
range through hurry up with now
serial relief arrays
whether or not there is anything to say
high lying scatter islands lead from behind
though we knew stars exist there in
despite light we break across the clouds
a way you can't remember
from what seems strange at first with
day's dog dancing under the finger tip
before heat drags everything indoors
behind an iron grating we make ourselves
at home in part of the way day seeps through
no matter how dark I do not throw off
my shadow errand wake to the
hour's draw upon us through this nowhere
suggesting winds that occupy the balcony
chairs tossed pillows rain tease
wash your face move out
pact with life ghosts hand back
over left shoulder to shape will longer than
expected where clarity
excludes her friction

head press infer steps proportion leans
destruction from a distance stake
in forever dreampaste disjunction rathers out of
where synapses midplace afternoon drive lethargy
a who she is old-fashioned placebo broods
dishevel morning skate surface aporias
where we room pad walls job stock
to treat you around ideas of wanting
mind feathers at outward pull from uncoached happiness
though champion should lists help do
you could have done better drags
a worry from the past carryall
of what is the worst that can happen net sift shred for
killer bee swarms along another country's check jam
prompts wake untouched by the natural
grown where you've planted resplay
watch out cause I'm being rebirth rooms
just outside the city's crest cleaner
refreshment centered in if I could roller coasters
and bridge mobile helpvan
bearing instachange photos from the upbeat of easy
always inflight charm glides
over the half buried seedcase
efficiency orbit jot norms
with walk restrained retrochic
prolonged burnout in)habits
night plane enclosures keep talking under
future hit wave synonymy we're okay practice
stands entering not yet at the edge

drawing a line through
where she speaks from bound(aries to remark
this universe we hear under
shard cluster discard reflect back
meet the compartment gaze head on
what kind of music you listen to directions
into the ring of the faxphone
with expected complaint brush we hide in
weightloss capital down from logic ladder sills
woo back surface through
red rock hike trail
tripping over nuts and bolts
morning aporia skate pond sunkinks
noise shift rush bows
in cliff swallow feeding flurry
to pin the cloak of our where from premise
a true fabric situates dazzle stitch work
electoral domain beeline scrape to discard variations
unknotting options under estranged trees
where fixed pleasure lies intersect
survey tabled love bird flight press
games undertaking as answer
until something checks throughout cleave
beckons off-ramp bumper string thrive stretch

scumbled graffiti prayer flag wall

completion surrenders understood as being

unable to find our way out from behind the arras

body drape hegemonies of you

create meanings according to your

road site de)construction cost sheet wanders in

who might enter that new mystic leap garden

and the where was I written from

park set aside in commodities' heroic tide pull

page breath inflate cord buttoning

sunlit parallelograms abraded blue roofs thumb

what you know is what you get to

clear more gap range

with how many feet in the word

and further reuse day launders

fusebreak labor resource looking national

and technoswings people like

stuck in what it meant

reflex passage questions underlie

out of your head into

arm reach alleging a question's print wag

or if paper and oranges conduct greetings as

an)other country above slate erasure memory

with no parallels to rest past

current rush hook and carry wheels invent us

pouring boxkite skies resist shapes emerge under

NINE AM

red carpet sieve over pound-shout radio constructs next door
schubert mask for crunch of feet gravelscape
music net above inside outside voices
wreathworks the skirl of air conditioner wheel to
slant my snapshot residence into high gloss from dust wake

conditions in place what I want out of reach
this hour feels like nine after nine after nine
since chemo over one-third of each day asleep and
more wished for even toward summer solstice
where private files of dawn scatter onto dialogue walkways

pink plastic blind slat truck-alarm fired, set off by passing cars
each word intoxicated, hungover, a crosshatch for examples
in how to put on this left cloth breast like a purpose to have
somewhere to go in a live fashion
today's early rose light ventures

close the west door against heat
a new house dog chews at the vinca and primrose
begging to be held, work day prepares a tally sheet screen
palms me through this field's opening
thin the sunflowers and squash, retie the tomatoes

secure entropy then butterfly stroke for a record test self identity on private or public policy just answer yes no or none of your business remember rural macho culture how grandfather talked to grandmother born into money she is the third woman at the table bring nature back to the city plant flowers it is important to be trapped in a hole where you can breathe explains probable cause is it a day behind or a day ahead presoccer mom body wax a gruesome suffering when you wear those clothes just figure out what to do then remember how we can't forget terror seized by panic a brown packet of photographs some faces beyond recognition bomb only when provoked zones infringe dozens of tornadoes spin off the slow moving eye a negative consequence to throw events in at that angle down home as

Ten AM

occasion's guise touch
topes dense charge weathers current
ted above below edge crimp
heaped

inset ice borne across floes
hold shed
blind effects gestate stand still
underego null open

street haven
mock adversity shadow clag
gift warning
wiser than yourself signals

wells
in)exhaustible
solidarity depth remember situates futile
hand draw rivermouth
separate

ask
two sides attune
riding apart resist regulate
stasis laughter elements
afterwards free float

day road
spread peeling native land skin
surrender
veracity adapts
refuses otherwise

ceaseless outwork confine
ideally flow but interrupted
destination energy
possible miss
inner keeps

breath force
wintertide
trust practice over
mirror pawn
discard ebb
clarity mediates

doubt lock
material case natures
real(ize stalk rustle
simple defense space

re)claim parts frontier
mundane thorn demon cling pause
collect deceive eye fasten
integrate

no proof mechanism first and last
lotus hooks to balance on
cylindrical teeth ruminate
recognition levels cool skin anchor
break minus sorrow

upend one unknown for another
the afterring to begin looks not at first
however arcane portraits
fool ties ready to hang you look
then willing to jump opens
dilate
enchantment crawls from the water
looking like that's ability to sit like this
lives almost circled as we see it
courses take on enough although others help

teleogaps pile together requisite engine
salt bed alleviates acute with chronic environment body easily misunderstood
look at the back first clearly invisible until far enough away
why not green ribbon afterimage good look sketches in red and white though not the obverse
lake water until desert hills bake ocher self reflection terminal crush by boat
stocked trout flesh the marinas row until water takes over
whether falls out of meaning weave said keep waiting turns out that way
let go let power chime help out again
energy banks picking at the sensory shroud
by other means shake immediate future works a current description
subtext in watch outs for not long term hand strike
pure once in a while charybdis level material
collect an under an over property stacks destroy how no and nothing depends upon
tiny transpersonal parts search for loss past shadowy
wait and do nothing grips the oneself within accomplishments
inspire fits hollowed fennel stalk stretching out most
all of it using into shade rust humors
TOMORROW dread cards free float too much said the way we've said
the confidence of not knowing needs to repeat again
insight collapse yet the break back motion feels new and better
not just another beautiful
landfills tissue
red rope wind ear rings
doubt lock also
obtains meaning

regard without goaled assault progress
compare and measure from that
follow with those lead
moments tune the gaze
for go somewhere shoal wrap

you're in remaining
enable world by itself reshapes
conditions when
real kairo warp
not to do your own despairs
ahead aside behind looks from detach
time this attitude on encroach
careless with after completion a similar time
it is all rage weep steer board
a vocabulary of way
to wear that dark red and bumping across the ground
fighting mode kicks in no where else to go
day's militance
flight song rhythms
no one increases ourself corrects the hold
sake / sake
to benefit the path guide dogs follow
rubble to reflect in
mental them
doing privilege whines

sway hold emotions
wave point reaches
organize you are
key according to diffusion
to be sure actions
endure slow and incorrect methods
to win a war employed by should
increases unresisting opaque
which persons experience rely on
places dwell in temporary lodging
to catch it games the field
open into outcome elements
blame retreats with a corpse wagon
an in comfort self interest
a family vest found states command
undergo inset threatens *wu wei*
prepare measures in which to hear
fence sturdy enough until gusts hit eighty
not an order I would have set out on slope
I can't so you'll have to where do those parts fit

in touch the body's environment
keep waiting says weave said we've
that out turn to depends upon
stay ahead of
immediate clockwork slips
betray as an honest self assurance
explore banked paving the suspended on
hour this downsized *portoir*
a fragrant sauce from yellow flowers
better and new agog
hold abandon repeat need then
to crave returns expecting to
road gestates over under
collect self for search parts transpersonals
nothing grips once you notice
cling down borne imagery
free float denizens
drop strive not by but of
insight this
the back looks pre)occupied
though leaved evenly
our space establishes by skip steps
the way to paves
dismiss untangled strands problems generate beginning
events pet food deer / dogs to drive
what is hold
what you're looking for zip life
create examples through outdraw
results inevitable where paths own turn

strive limits cannot
hand in front personality brattice
first love then practice
letting safe feel sharks nearby
what are those life buoys we long for
lead attitudes that must
what appetites the only here
blue shine after black matte lake
mistakes making years later understand
near swim where it's still fresh

gruel toward hunger preface

burst drain

a color of shellfish
choir bleed blanket spelling

agnail stand rend fast

sense change

passage angst call case

her hair flame chased

perfectbound morning thread climb

sea room pitch and roll
lawful air leg spin

right now

open shed shoeing forge

resource gaps hurl wire rout labret
an ornament for the lips

fine sink totter elaborates
circadian

scored opposites
day timbre
where memory sits down

hearth
shapelit
window stain

air heat tear fragrant

conscious wall   blue numen breech life

umbel happenings   umbra tuft

flat plate dual parapet

what else

outside echofires from where

full serif   half serif

shore carried between them

lie down on

what then decides

hand over pledges own

sweet sour along energy

juniper tea steep after curtain   result chain

impulse yucca leaf whine

blue repels loud quarreling

barrage model

murk billow doorway tread

left right without knots

prize harbor bite click

red rouge marrow smear

cloth measures and cuts

burial charm sac receipt

simples them with us
          groundspill
                    house beam
                       lace cap froth garden
                              reconstellate
                         hear and now selects
                    textrose   ,weathertext
unconsidered givens beneath which pole star
     gauze lift minium tongue morning
     winter arc turns lower   abbreviating
     dawn's abacus and plastic flute dissemble

residential flocked sequiturs along toplined trees
  toast crackle energy edge tether
    right from here into day long rush to speak for
   not quite purchases   bondaging   how difference might rather
 nervous surface skip trajectory atmosphere fuses the skin

                    vast yesterday despite stream
               follow out of speed bank fester into
                    meanwhile modular selvings
imprint song nest rods   fledgling crest flutter surfeits
          as a matted dog crosses that north corner of yard

experience windowed in counterclockwise sundial shadow lines
     a borderland tag becoming
  not the bird who likes to loosen a snare, then fasten it again
to show off her strange new skill
through many ways atrium entry begins today terrain

like morning in too strong coffee laminate crepe myrtle leans through always more too late arrives nothing more or less than I began with or how this means after great cycles of music and silent sift counter

so here's the rule: zeroes divisible by four unless divisible by 400 lead a world to leap second corrections until festivals re)fix

random walks choose somewhat for necessary conditions
indeed results show numerical howevers branch
we conjecture birth and death chains might where
computer fits range >=< mutations become
possibility admits >=< probability to denote
meantime define(s
systems fact functional relations] *WHERE NOTHING MIGHT OCCUR* [

call the left hand side matrix] *EMPTY LUMINOUS* [
identity equivalent represents transition or secular multiplicity
use the fact that systems become
conditions boundary process duration
a tail converges toward last inequality as furthermore

hypotheses of then for every is almost certain
obtain and apply similar fashions transient and recurrent with drift
finitely often supposes only
no other transitions are allowed] *SOMEPLACE* [
we take all successive returns as strictly positive so that

an arbitrary second proof exists if we define hurry to assume given
other possible states >=< being empty closed
iterate the number understood
type the sample sequence considering time's up indicator sounds
otherwise as trivial
countable notes fix bivariate
] *ANY MOMENT INTERSTICES DISAPPEAR* [
this chain is called the process of
or im)properly essential set(s
variables discrete and random adapt
forest >=< thicket >=< hedge
a system of equations finds the measure
to accept in)transient >=< in)variant
state space enters the closure
abstract >=<integral
positive >=< null

a dichotomy in force can be shown to guarantee almost
choose attribute sweep]*TRIP BEAM* [
transition kernel >=< model
state space >=< finite
identify a sequence of environments absorbing initial heat without full knowledge
count and multiply by climate quadrants
joint range unaware activates] *DESIRE PROOF NOTES TO* [

straw burst settles
how she identifies
day axle
vigilant skin
shirt vocabulary
occasional shaping
take care market
media peer
shape events thinner huge faces perfect
buildings to implode later
cumbersome staging toward someone with whom we know

identify known to destabilize closing kiss
already says where ,censor ,defy
romance woundcurve noise omission

tears rend forward
exude utter fluence
privatus privy to something within an other
salt liqueur
compress a lot of withs
testimony *within* oneself ,facts viewed under

fourteen hour days too often with noiseband along treadmill eloquents how far can you chronic like other gapful shorthands light penciled in where negative space betweens us with outrage off the diving board then breaststroke on digital file where still fresh idioms for machine construing cumulative I give you all my U TURNS and you want more now in grass too high junk out long term zoo are we ready surfaces from primitive light flare right-now darlings in seven minutes or it is lost retrieval tractors letting too much passes our common home market resourcing orangewood frames worked to well-shaped window stains where backdrop weighs in by perseid tear bath or textimony long-term trapdoors reconstellate this warming cycle socked in to oversummer remote with we don't quite match rhythms in have not words what you begin to mean over power lunch sound room rattles just change your sense of balmy a larger receipt envelope uptimes
for anything to be hungry needs a chance

subtraction speeds up

it isn't about appearances corrects itself

until is not what you remember

wine razor prescription call mail

one hour photographs ,tree and earth auger

anchorscape make something of it frontiers

being from fabrics assembled

before naming what is faithful description

rote scale in which frame appears

what have we not altered

~~altared by touch~~

intended or not the site(s explain

edge monumental

forebodes if it matters so much

where it becomes the idea of itself intersection slams

where lives fall around us in love with

~~objects~~

soften gaze pose

moth light

as though one contour line denotes the struggle and who holds the line between tide marks

palms face outward so fingers can interlace

slowly bend backward ,bend forward

farther than illustrated in variations of extreme

fix gaze at the back of your hands

exchange the words right and left

mind wanders

try again pauses

continue slow lowering

repeat in continuous motion

raise upper body hold light and hollow

in soles of the feet concentrate

diagram out of your mind
((nuclear plant chillers counteract warming ,tone ~~it~~ down))
words happen to the body
fix begin and where to fall as part of the circle
an instant's own aura of belonging
,diverse ,facile
so much depends exactly in between
don't get ~~it~~ rejects
always another level crossovers area
chance change draws long periods of time compress
although night is not required
misread through domains ladder
explain smiling how you feel
different systems kind
naming names you sound initiates by phoneme fragment rubbed around on the tongue
strung ,plucked
this last not likely
one problem subways toward able to want re(considered life expects that provising another's golden not so fortunate in challenges you withstand too much wanting to be there already and failure to notice teeth spar spadework stick fly downdrill bend might game tilt scuffle vie horse stitch uphill punch scrape drag plug grind shoot daunt wear wait temper stand quick resist duel quarry spectacle absents also filled in options thought through not so fast
ripcurrent layers
seizure whistle and call
with between among of an the while
a slate path ,convexing

nothing moment spherelike swallowed with what's here on fitting possibility to follow grows everything upward someplace insignial and she framing imaginal breath so anteroom to not see crux beam order an empty wait market a trajectory getting onto limitless any roadway capture your own proof cling ready notes merge by if interstice re)turns or song walls dis)appear waiting inlet set to desire persona she must do of or how(ever our then imagines turn back level luminous over from and in eggshell deflecting points with retrench seen empty of ask cut away to now hero I phase barrage tossed in touchstone spew forever trip

of silent

and beige carpet power null float

open slipping sky nature to recover as in consequent

at first an event of time

separating out denotes an area of extension

as in a gelatin print shelter abridgement

refractive past

interim completion chases

advance traversal

woven sedge in almond or jade

acid sea sail curtain

cloud chamber cirrostratus overcast soft brush

corn flag float bundle

along across water furrows

bound wing slough

aperture
admit to opening weathers
vowel
unobstructing sound conducts
as lips without key, slide, or piston

gap texture
unconcealed quaquaversal
to court as property, annex, or claim
enough nicely seems an order
deciduary margins line in
decolored bird down
to indicate limit serves offward action
defense prohibits forbid
a passage in the photograph surfacing
argument to hear local hoops and letters
suppose choice reasons
they will each time a little differently
a
and what you use words for
tremendous diminishing the other side
long-term discontent gestate frame
ask her about vague sense
the conservationist
finish process appeals through
cope coverage following up crises

reverse continuum effect draws further into view
set to stun until someone you know
preparation removal relates
anecdotal risk deal
whatever results why
example millimeter
err breath takes up lets go
hit upon intervals manage a lucid pool
terribly undertaken sometimes to underscore property
music fanned refusing current descriptions of sky
reckoned evidence and true dilute unexplained elements
nothing is usually symbolic
like any part of life's fecund emptiness
where surface fails
permitting seasons reconcile
a meantime territory
unburdened
where stretch forward alludes
somehow said quite the way interference orchestrates
blowdry ten or natural disturbance event morning in plain air fulcrum push and pull